WOMEN OF FAITH INTERCESSORY PRAYER MANUAL

A Guide to Starting an Intercessory Prayer Line

By

Minister Vanessa Jackson

Author/Publisher Info

Unless otherwise indicated, all Scripture quotations are taken from the *King James Version* of the Bible.

WOMEN OF FAITH
Intercessory Prayer Manual

A Guide to Starting an Intercessory Prayer Line
Copyright © 2011 by Vanessa Jackson

Women of Faith Prayer Ministries
P.O. Box 642
Park Forest, IL. 60466

ISBN: 978-0-9849360-7-6

Library of Congress Control Number: 2012941247

Printed in the United States of America
All rights reserved under International Copyright Law. Contents and/or cover may not be reproduced in whole or in part in any form without the express written consent of the Author/Publisher.

Dedication

Dedicated to all the Women & Men of Faith Prayer Intercessors

Taconna Hazzard
Lolita Alston
Arnetta Roberts
Louella Jamerson
Bertriece Hughes
Gwendolyn Hawkins
Thelma Stroud
Alice Roberts
Kimberly Morris
Lisa Green
Rachel Hawkins
Jasmine Roberts
Merilee Rhoden
Lesia Rucker
Minister Vernon Alston
William T. Jackson

These Women and Men of God are dedicated intercessors interceding on behalf of others on a weekly basis.

Table of Contents

Dedication iii
Table of Contents v
Foreword 7
Origin 8
INTRODUCTION 9
Chapter One: What is Intercession? 11
Notes 15
Chapter Two: What does it take to be an Intercessor? 17
Notes 23
Chapter Three: Starting Your Intercessory Prayer Line 25
Notes 28
Chapter Four: Facilitating the Prayer Line 29
Notes 33
Chapter Five: Caring For Your Body 35
Notes 36
My Prayer Line Experiences and Rewards 37
Notes 39
CONCLUSION 41
Notes 43
CONTACT: 45

Foreword

Minister Vanessa Jackson, President of the "Women of Faith Prayer Ministries", first I begin by saying "thank you" for allowing me to be part of your Intercessory Prayer Manual and what God is doing in your life.

I have always known that God's hand was upon you for a great work, and I am excited to see it unfold for such a time as this. With so many things going on in this world, for you to be a prayer warrior and intercessor is great, however, to be able to instruct and teach others how to be an intercessor is even greater!

My prayer for you is that God will continue to bless you as you move forward in the ministry that He has called you to.

Again, I am so honored to write this forward and applaud my dear friend and fellow minister of the gospel. Without doubt, I know that this prayer manual will be a great blessing to all who read it.

Yours in Christ.

Elder Annie S. Owens
President of Monument of Faith Church Women's Ministry

Origin

The Lord called Vanessa Jackson to the ministry as an anointed Teacher and Prophetess; in doing so He gave her these two scriptures, St. John 15:16 and Jeremiah 1:5, as the foundation for His call upon her life. She was licensed as a Minister of the Gospel under Apostle Richard D. Henton.

Minister Vanessa Jackson, is the Founder of Women of Faith Prayer Ministries, which began as a prayer line in 2000, with a few women praying via 3-way calling on their individual telephones. Over the years the prayer line grew to include women from other cities and states calling to experience the power of prayer.

Through the guidance of the Holy Ghost Minister Vanessa was inspired to change the prayer line to a prayer ministry, now nationally known as Women of Faith Prayer Ministries. The ministry's motto is "We Believe in the Power of Prayer!" Minister Vanessa does not take lightly the mantle of intercessory prayer and the training of other Intercessors God has given her, as she firmly believes in the power of prayer to change lives and circumstances.

The Women of Faith Intercessory Prayer Ministries has grown over the years, with women calling from various cities and states across the country.

On June 9, 2008, under the guidance and direction of the Holy Spirit the ministry began having live conference prayer lines, which allowed a larger number of women to call in at one time.

This intercessory manual was created to provide a guide line for future intercessors and trainers.

INTRODUCTION

By Vanessa Jackson

Amidst all of the things we do to nurture and maintain an intimate relationship with God, prayer is the most essential. It is our life line and our effectiveness in all that we attempt to do for Him is only as strong and as deep as our prayer lives and communication with Him. It is only through prayer and God's word that we learn who we really are in Christ. The more time we spend yielding in prayer, the more the Holy Ghost can empower and anoint us as intercessors.

If we are to be the anointed intercessors that God is seeking in this hour we must recognize how vitally important it is to pray in the Spirit. Romans 8:26 emphasizes this: *"Likewise the Spirit also helpeth our infirmities: for we know not what we should pray for as we ought: but the spirit itself maketh intercession for us with groanings which cannot be uttered. 27 And he that searcheth the hearts knoweth what is the mind of the Spirit, because he maketh intercession for the saints according to the will of God. (KJV)*

The same is true for beginning an intercessory prayer line; you must be lead by the wisdom and discernment of the Holy Spirit in the selection and training of intercessors as well as interceding on your prayer line.

Intercessory prayer is a ministry which carries great responsibility and tremendous reward. It is a blessing to be able to posture one's self to be used by the Holy Ghost to pray in behalf of others. As a child of God, we have a direct hotline to God and at any given time we can go boldly to the throne of grace to obtain the help needed.

As an intercessor and beginning an intercessory prayer line should not be taken lightly. We have been given the power to loose and bind here on earth, with our heavenly Father backing

us up. Interceding is standing in the gap or between the people and/or circumstances
and praying that the Lord will interrupt the plans of the enemy for their life and situation.

An intercessory prayer line can have a tremendously positive impact in and on the lives of those who will call in for prayer, as well as in the life of the intercessor. With the Holy Ghost it is a win-win situation. It is our prayer that this manual will guide, inspire and enlighten you as you begin an intercessory prayer line ministry. Prayer is always in order and demand in this day and hour.

This manual is prayerfully written to serve as a guideline and foundation, upon which you may build your intercessory prayer line ministry, and not just to build it but take it to the next level through your yielding and the empowerment of the Holy Ghost.

-Minister Vanessa Jackson

Chapter One: What is Intercession?

Intercession- is an act or instance of interceding; Pleading on behalf of another; entreaty in favor of another, especially a prayer or petition to God in behalf of another.

Intercede: *To go or come between two parties; to plead before one them on behalf of the other.*

Intercession is a form of petition; it is petitioning God in the place of another. Intercession is also a prayer that pleads with God, not only for your needs but the needs of others as well. Intercession involves yielding to the Holy Spirit as you pray God's will for someone or some situation, refusing to let it go until his will comes to pass.

Intercession is warfare. As we pray and come before the Father we are strengthened and empowered to do battle in the Spirit realm.

Warfare: *Means to weaken or destroy another; struggle between competing entities. Military operations between enemies; Struggle for superiority or victory.*

But the battleground is not of this earth. The Bible says we are not fighting against humans. *"For we wrestle not against flesh and blood, but against principalities, against powers, against the rulers of the darkness of this world, against spiritual wickedness in high places"* (Ephesians. 6:12, KJV).

This means Satan is constantly using people to carry out his dirty work. There are demonic spirits that try to come against God's people to distract and deter them from what God has promised them, or told them to do as well as to prevent men and women from coming to Christ.

As Christians, when we pray and intercede we engage in a spiritual warfare against the devil. We are soldiers and warriors in the army of the Lord, therefore, we must utilize all of the spiritual weapons God's word and the Holy Spirit makes available to us.

What are our spiritual weapons?

Prayer: *an address (as a petition) to God in word or thought; a set order of words used in praying: an earnest request or wish; the act or practice of praying to God (kneeling in prayer); a religious service consisting chiefly of prayers —often used in plural; something prayed for.*

Through prayer we have access to God's power source that enables us to overcome seemingly impossible obstacles. It brings the power from on high into our lives and nothing shall be impossible as we pray in faith. Consistent prayer causes us to foster many positive experiences in and with God. It is our job to pray and intercede but the results are up to the Holy Ghost.

Praise: *to commend, to applaud or magnify; to express a favorable judgment of; to glorify God, to express praise; For the Christian, praise is lifting up and glorifying the Lord, a humbling of ourselves with heartfelt expressions of thanksgiving, adoration and admiration.*

The Bible says that *God inhabits in the praises of His people (Psalms 22:3)*. This means God *"dwells"* in the atmosphere created by His praise. In other words, praise isn't simply something we do because we've come into His presence; Praise is the vehicle of faith that actually brings us into God's presence and power. Praise and worship is the *"backstage pass"*, if you will, which allows us entrance to the place of His glory. The psalmist declares we should, *"Enter into his gates with thanksgiving, and into his courts with praise: be thankful unto him, and bless his name"* (Psalms 100:4).

Worship: *reverence offered a divine being or supernatural power; also an act of expressing such reverence; a form of religious practice with its creed and ritual; extravagant respect or admiration for, devotion; refer to a posture of submission and the acknowledgment of God's sovereignty.*

Worship is a more powerful tool than we as Saints can imagine. It has the power to change atmospheres, hearts, minds and certainly impact the heart and movement of God. True worship always brings the Presence of God on the scene in our behalf.

Word of God:

The Word of God is a guide and tool that we use to be instructed in the way that the Lord will have us to live our daily lives. In prayer it gives us the pattern to pray and how to intercede for others. The word teaches us how to love and have compassion for our brothers and sisters in Christ. It first, shows us ourselves to make sure that our lives line up with God's word. The Word is part of our foundation to stand and depend on.
"For the word of God is quick (alive), and powerful (active, energizing) and sharper than any two-edged sword, piercing even to the dividing asunder of soul and spirit, and of the joints and marrow (adequately proclaiming what man ought to be and can only be in Christ), and is a discerner of the thoughts and intents of the heart."(Hebrews 4:12, KJV Expository Study Bible)

Praying in the Spirit (Speaking in Tongues):

Praying and speaking in tongues edifies us, it also allows the Holy Spirit to express Himself when we don't know how to pray as we ought. He makes intercession for us according to God's will for our lives and circumstances. The Holy Ghost is our Equalizer when it comes to spiritual warfare, despite spiritual discernment, we still don't see everything that is coming against us in the realm of the spirit. Therefore, praying in tongues is a valuable weapon that should be utilized each time we enter into His presence and engage in spiritual warfare. When we speak in tongues the devil doesn't know what we are saying, so it confuses the enemy. The tongues are one of the evidences of being filled with the Holy Spirit which is a gift from God.

Holy Ghost: is the third party of the trinity (Father, Son and the Holy Ghost) He is a Comforter, Guide, Counselor, Teacher,

Revealer, Discerner, and One who warns and convicts. The Holy Ghost comes with power of attorney to use the name of Jesus when we pray.

Intercessory prayer takes place in this spiritual world where the battles for our own lives, our families, our friends and our nation are won.

God can do so much through yielded and anointed prayer. Prayer and intercession is important to God, so much so, that He gave the Holy Ghost to help us and to ensure that we are effective.

Notes

Notes

Chapter Two: What does it take to be an Intercessor?

"Prayer is simply talking to God. He speaks to us; we listen. We speak to Him; He listens. A two-way process: speaking and listening. The more you pray, the easier it becomes. The easier it becomes, the more you'll pray." Mother Teresa

"The primary means by which God's will is to be done here on earth is by prayer. It is an astounding fact that the destiny of events has been placed in the hands of praying men (women). If we pray for God's will to be done, it will be done! If we don't pray for His will to be done, the devil will have his way." (Excerpt 'Ask, Seek, Knock Bible Study')

Discipline in prayer is essential for every Christian, especially anyone who desires to be an Intercessor. *Discipline: a rule or system of rules governing conduct or activity; training that corrects, molds, or perfects; control gained by obedience or training.* Being disciplined in prayer does not mean that you have to be on your knees 24/7 however, you must have a prayerful mindset 24/7. You always want to stay connected to the Father.

Becoming an intercessor:

Intercessors must prevail in prayer, persistence is always the key.

Jesus reinforces this in Luke 11: 9 saying *"And I say unto you, Ask, and it shall be given you; seek, and ye shall find; knock, and it shall be opened unto you." (KJV)* Intercessors will keep asking, keep seeking, and keep knocking. E. M. Bounds said: "Intercessors never prepare to quit praying until the answer comes."

In order for one to become effective as an Intercessor you must adhere to the following:

1. Be Persistent in Prayer: The effectual fervent prayer of a righteous man availeth much." (James 5:15, KJV) Persistence means continuance of an effort or in prayer, especially in spite of opposition, obstacles, or discouragement. An intercessor must be able to remain consistent and persistent in prayer and not fall victim to discouragement and inconsistency.

- **A.** **Pray:** You must be a person who is given over to prayer. *"Men ought to always pray..."(Luke 18:1, KJV)*
- **B.** **Seek:** It is imperative as an Intercessor that you seek the directive will of God as you pray. *"Seek first the kingdom of God..." (Matthew 6:33-34, KJV)*
- **C.** **Ask:** Always ask for the wisdom and direction of the Holy Ghost as you proceed into prayer. *"If any of you lack wisdom, let him ask of God,...(James 1:5; "...for we know not what we should pray for as we ought:...Romans 8:26, KJV)*
- **D.** **Wait**: In your spirit you are prepared to wait on the peace and assurance of God regarding the person or situation for which you are praying. *"So shall my word be that goeth forth..."(Isaiah 55:11)*

2. Surrender – To yield to the power, control or possession of another upon compulsion or demand; to give up completely or agree to forgo especially in favor of another.

- **A.** Yield- to surrender or submit oneself to another
- **B.** Get in the spirit
- **C.** Trust in the Lord-(Proverbs 3:5)
- **D.** Listen to the voice of the Lord, whatever word or prophecy that he may want to use you to say to individuals on the prayer line.

3. Distractions- *to draw or direct one's attention in a different direction; to stir up or confuse with conflicting emotions or motives.* As an Intercessor there may be certain circumstances that may arise in your personal life, which the enemy may try to use, which would make you feel unqualified to pray for others. For example:

- **A.** Lack of Finances

B. Marriage/Family issues
C. Loss of job
D. Illness (i.e. sickness in your own body.)
E. Equipment failure.

When distractions of this magnitude come upon an intercessor you should not stop praying but continue to trust and believe on behalf of others as well as for yourself. Bind the hand of the enemy bringing distractions in your personal life and those for whom you are praying. Plead the Blood of Jesus for there is power in the blood. Use your spiritual weapons against the attack of the enemy. Continue to stand on God's word and his promises and wait on the fulfillment of those promises. Continue to praise and worship the Lord and be a leader to compel others to do the same.

The importance of All Intercessors being filled with the Holy Ghost:

The Holy Ghost is a magnificent Gift from God. He is not only a Comforter, a Guide, and Instructor, but the ultimate Helper and Teacher for us as we pray and intercede in behalf of others. The Holy Ghost will bring to your remembrance the promises and directives from God's word as to how and what we should pray for.

As an intercessor we rely totally upon the Holy Ghost to speak to and through us as we pray. We need the power and the holy boldness He brings to be effective. In addition, we need to be in tune with and know the voice of the Lord to move as He speaks. Intercession is such an important work in the Lord so we have to be right on target and having the Holy Ghost will enable us to be our maximum for the Lord. He is a rejuvenator and charge for the people of God.

New intercessors:

When the Lord speaks to you about adding new intercessors, you want to make sure that they are comfortable enough to let the Holy Ghost direct them as they intercede on behalf of others. They will be launching out into new surroundings in the spirit. The prayer lines draw many people in need of prayer so you don't want to overwhelm them with trying to pray for all callers on the line, especially if you have a large number of people on the line.

Therefore, we suggest that as they begin praying on the line, another seasoned intercessor prays along with them. One can start the prayer off and the other one can finish where they left off. This way they will get use to the flow and can ease into it gradually.
We want to keep them encouraged and strengthened in their faith to believe they can do all things through Christ who gives them the strength.

It is essential to meet with the new intercessors to explain to them about the structure of the prayers, and the basics of facilitating a prayer session. You can also ask them what they feel more comfortable with, as far as starting or ending the prayer.

Becoming an intercessor is a two-fold blessing. **First**, you have the privilege to freely give of yourself to the Lord to pray for others; despite your own personal matters or battles. **Second**, it will elevate you in your faith because you believe for others to be saved, healed, set free and delivered. Intercessory prayer will usher you to another level in the Lord and in your own prayer life. You will draw strength and determination as you pray. As you begin to hear the powerful testimonies and praise reports you will increase in your faith.
As a new Intercessor it would be a wise to get quiet before the Lord.

We also recommend that you put together a schedule for your intercessors. This will be such a great tool to have to spread out the intercessor so that they don't get overwhelmed each week. It also, brings structure to your prayer ministry.

Training your Intercessors:

It is extremely important that you adequately train your intercessors in both your vision and mission for your

Intercessory Prayer line, as well as how to properly facilitate the prayer line. You want to establish a pattern of excellence and uniformity in and for your ministry. Clear and proper training minimizes the potential for chaos, disruptions and misunderstanding.

Training involves clearly defining and articulating your goals and expectations for intercessors and their performance each time they greet your callers on the line. In addition, it is a good idea to have monthly meetings for updates, changes, new direction from the Lord and simply to maintain that everyone has a clear and concise understanding and are functioning on the same page. It is *your* responsibility as the Founder, Director or Leader to make sure your intercessors are trained and equipped to get the job done for the glory of God. Also, to provide necessary follow-up to maintain excellence and consistency and professionalism on your line.

In addition, you may want to schedule a separate day and meeting specifically for your intercessors to pray over them and their respective needs/requests. This will also provide you an opportunity to interactive with your intercessors and address any concerns they may have.

Guarding the anointing:

1 John 2:27 "But the ANOINTING which ye have received of him abideth in you, and ye need not that any man teach you: but as the same ANOINTING teacheth you of all things, and is truth, and is no lie, and even as it hath taught you, ye shall abide in him."

As an intercessor you have to guard the anointing in your life. You have to be very careful to keep your temple clean, to have clean conversations, be sensitive of the environments you allow yourself to be part of and to be in tune with God at all times.

As an intercessor you have to guard the anointing in your life. You have to be very careful to keep your temple clean, to have clean conversations and to be in tune with God at all times.

1 Corinthians 6:19 *"What? know ye not that your body is the TEMPLE of the Holy Ghost [which is] in you, which ye have of God, and ye are not your own?"*

We must not be carnal that the Lord can't depend on us to pray at the drop of hat. We have to be available when called upon. We can't be unequally yoked and around things or people that is not pleasing unto the Lord. We don't need a decrease of God's anointing but an increase of his anointing. Guard the anointing that God has given you. The anointing is to break yokes and set the captives free it is no goodness of your own. Don't take the anointing for granted.

We must have clean conversations and to be in tune with God at all times. We must not be carnal, relating to or given into fleshly pleasures and appetites, which could cause you not to be spiritual minded to pray when the Lord needs to pray on behalf of others. We have to be available when called upon.

Notes

Notes

Chapter Three: Starting Your Intercessory Prayer Line

If you've decided you would like to intercede on behalf of others by starting your own telephone prayer line, here are a few suggestions to help get you started and be successful:
We cannot emphasize enough the importance of having the right equipment.

Equipment

A reliable phone service and telephone, preferably a phone with a headset jack are a necessity in order for your callers to be able to clearly hear the prayer and/or whatever word may be released to them. If you conduct your prayer session while on speaker phone, it is important that you stay close to the phone, especially if you are prone to walk around as you pray. This may cause you to go out of range and your callers may not hear you clearly or at all.

It is not recommended that cell phones be used to conduct prayer sessions, as they are too unpredictable and depending on where you are, may be prone to distortion and interference, as well as signal loss and dropped calls. You want to avoid these kinds of distractions as much as possible.

It is wise to invest in a good headset so that you may be able to move around while praying and maintain the clarity of the call.

The importance of being heard by everyone is very vital. We know that sometimes the enemy will try to bring distractions whether it is on a telephone prayer line or praying in person, but we have to make sure they we do everything possible to keep our listeners able to hear the prayers that are going up on their behalf. If you are on the phone make sure your cordless phone is charged and that you are in a quiet place praying without any distractions around you.

There are a number free conference call services available on the internet.

Here are 3 free services that you can sign up with in order to start a prayer conference line where multiple people can dial in at the same time. You would also enjoy the benefits of being able to record schedule prayers.

1. FreeConference.com
2. MyFreeconferenceline.com
3. Freeconferencingcalling.com

Prayer Line Growth

When your prayer line begins to increase in callers, it is good to pray and ask the Lord for wisdom on how to accommodate and pray for the larger number of callers. *Proverbs 3:5, 6 says: "Trust in the Lord with all your heart; and lean not unto your own understanding. In all your ways acknowledge Him, and He shall direct your paths."*

You may desire to pray in depth or specifically for each and every caller, but you have to use wisdom for this can be very taxing on you physically as well as the callers, you will need to be time conscience. You don't want to extend your prayer sessions so long that callers will begin to get weary because of the length of the calls.

You may have started out praying for each person individually and fervently however, when the line increases, if you yield, the Lord will give you a more effective way of praying if you ask him.

Instead of praying for individual requests you can categorize requests in groups such as*:* **healing, finances, family, salvation etc.**

The Vision

Habakkuk 2:2, 3 says: *"And the Lord answered me, and said, write the vision, and make it plain upon tables that he may run who reads it. For the vision is yet for an appointed time, but at the end it shall speak, and not lie: though it tarry, wait for it; because it will surely come, it will not tarry."*

Hold on to the vision that God has given you. Stay prayerful, so that your eyes and ears are open. The devil comes to kill, steal and destroy your vision. Sometimes he will use people to interrupt, discourage or try to deter you away from what God has given you to do. Ask God for wisdom and discernment, because His Spirit is a discerner of motives and intents of the heart.

Family: Family is important to God. A family is a group of people who are important to each other and offer each other love and support, especially in times of crises.

Many people equate ministry with their relationship with God. There is a difference. There is no compromise when it comes to your relationship with God, you are His child. Ministry is just an assignment that God has added to your life, it is not who you are it's what you do. Ministry should never be allowed to impinge upon your family relationships. If you are married you got married to your spouse to build a life *not* to build a ministry.

It is important that you prioritize your prayer ministry. God's priorities are as follows: God first, family next, job or career and then ministry. If any one of those is out of place you are not in line with His priorities.

Jesus said in John 10:10 *"The thief comes not, but for to steal, and to kill, and to destroy: I am come that they might have life, and that they might have it more abundantly."* The devil loves to destroy the family unit; therefore, we must use wisdom in making sure that we are doing what is expected of us to protect our family relationships. Your family is your life *not* the ministry. We build a life with our families and loved ones. You *serve* in ministry as an assignment given through leadership.

Notes

Chapter Four: Facilitating the Prayer Line

Now that you have decided that you want to begin an Intercessory Prayer Line here is a sample guideline you may use to open and conduct your prayer session. As the Moderator of the prayer session, please note that, most Conference Calling Services provide a different number or code for you than what your callers will use. **(Do not give this to callers!)**

Opening the call: As the Lead Intercessor for the call it is extremely important that you are on the line **at least 3 to 5 minutes** before your callers.

Lead Intercessor: Greet your callers by saying "Hi this is _____ welcome to the *ex: Women of Faith Prayer line.* Who's on the line?" *(You will usually hear a beep or chime when a new caller comes on the line.)* **NOTE: Always have a cheerful, warm, respectful, and welcoming tone of voice when greeting your callers.**

If the caller doesn't state their name when they come on the line ask for it.

After receiving callers name proceed to ask them if they have a prayer request. Write down their name and briefly list the prayer request. It is essential to have a notebook or pad for listing names and prayer requests, also to have the names and requests available to pray over at a later time.

Repeat this procedure until you have greeted all callers and received all requests on the line.

You should not have side conversations about administrative things while you are facilitating a prayer and other callers are on the line. You want to conduct the prayer line in a professional manner. If you have any **questions** regarding the codes or if you are to pray on that day or evening please ask your questions offline via email or text please.

You never want to quench the spirit, if you feel that the Lord is moving you want to flow in the spirit, which could be some ones breakthrough.

Basic Structure

Provide a scripture for the call as the lead intercessor or you may select another individual to read a scripture that the Lord has laid on their heart. If you choose someone else to provide the scripture, it is a good thing to ask them ahead of time that they may be prepared. You always want to conduct your prayer line in the spirit of excellence and have things done intelligently and in an orderly manner.

To assure that you have accounted for all the callers, verbally go back over your list, asking if you have every one's name and prayer request.

Using music on the line

A recorded song may be presented by the lead intercessor or you may feel led to call upon someone on the line to render a song. (If possible **please** try to notify the individual, **in advance**, that you would like them to render a song). This prevents awkward moments. Also, if you are presenting a recorded song it is a good thing to make sure the volume is loud enough for callers to hear the song clearly. *Songs should be no longer than 5 minutes.*

Muting Callers and Recording

It is now time to mute all callers and set for recording. Let your callers know that you are about to mute them and begin to record.

Depending upon which Conference Calling Service you selected you will press: *(prompts will vary based upon service selected.)*
*2 to hear how many callers are actually on the line
*5 to mute out all callers *(Individual callers mute themselves by *6)*

*8 to mute out ring sounds of callers entering a call or leaving.
*9 will set for recording prompting you to enter recording number which would be the date of the call example: 05-12-10. *(*9 again to end recording.)*

It is up to your discretion as to whether you want to mute your callers before or after you read the scripture and present the song.

Structure to start prayer:

A. Always open up with Praise and Worship to God.
B. General Repentance covering everyone to make sure there is no hindrance or interference to the flow of the Holy Spirit or the prayer getting through.
C. Pray for callers as the Lord directs you.

*Be sensitive to the Holy Ghost while praying for each person.

*Use wisdom when there are over 10 callers on the line and also verbalizing certain personal aspects in a person's life.

*The entire prayer session should last approximately one (1) hour and 15 minutes after gathering names and requests, but not quenching the spirit, if the Holy Ghost is moving in a particular manner that cannot be disrupted.

Ask a caller you are very familiar and comfortable with to do the closing prayer. It is even better to have a closer designated *before* your session, if this is possible. After they pray you can press ***5** until you hear "*all callers are **unmuted**.*" At which point you can ask if anyone dialed in after the prayer started. Also, you may open the floor to anyone who may have a praise report, or something the Lord put on their heart to share. Be sure to instruct callers to try to keep comments brief.

Maintaining control on the line:

You must always do your best to maintain control and courtesy on the line. At times, during the beginning or ending of a prayer session when all lines are <u>unmuted</u>, people may have a tendency to engage in side conversations or have other things going on in the back ground that can be disruptive. During those times politely and calmly ask people to **press #6 to mute themselves out** in order to maintain order, reverence and respect on the line, and especially for the presence of God.

Remember, the facilitator has the responsibility to, and you are in charge of the call, as well as maintaining the atmosphere.

<u>Announcements:</u> If your ministry has a designated announcer you may ask them to present any ministry related announcements.

<u>Ending the prayer:</u> If there are no further comments, end the call by thanking everyone For calling in and saying God bless them until you speak with them again.

You want to try to keep the line hollowed out and not linger on the line after the prayer has finished, and remarks and announcements have been given.

Notes

Notes

Chapter Five: Caring For Your Body

It is crucial that intercessors take care of their physical bodies as tremendous strength and energy can be expended when you are engaged in intense, Spirit-led intercession or travailing in prayer on behalf of others.

You have to make sure that you keep your body properly hydrated by drinking enough water and fluids that prevent dehydration. After a strenuous prayer session you may be drenched, therefore, it is best to have a change of clothing so that you do not catch cold. You may also have a cup of herbal tea with lemon and honey for your throat to preserve it. You can also have cough drops handy for after praying.

It is important to practice healthy eating habits, a balance daily meal with fruits and vegetables to preserve your body. We recommend exercise of some sort whether it is going to the gym once or twice a week or daily walking, whatever is best for you in order to maintain stamina.

We *must* take care of the body given to us by God, it is the only means by which we can accomplish His will and carry out His assignment on our lives. God expects us to use wisdom in all areas of our lives, especially when it comes to being and staying healthy for His glory.

Although Paul said in **1 Timothy 4:8** "...for bodily exercise is profitable for a little; but godliness is profitable for all things, having promise of the life which now is, and of that which is to come."(ASV)

Basically Paul was telling us the primary emphasis of our lives should not be on taking pride in developing our bodies only, as the Greeks did during his time. However, we should work to develop both body and spirit, for the spirit is the eternal part of us. Yet we need healthy bodies to house our spirit man in order for us to work and be effective in what we are called to do as intercessors.

Notes

My Prayer Line Experiences and Rewards

As an intercessor for the Women of Faith Prayer Ministries it has been a very exciting and wonderfully rewarding experience. It affords me the opportunity to put my own needs and desires aside and intercede on behalf of others. Since its inception I have seen the prayer line grow from one night of prayer to day and night prayer times on a weekly basis. The experience of speaking and interacting with different women and men across the nation is such an honor.

The numerous testimonies that we hear on a weekly basis is even more gratifying, because I believe in the power of prayer. To hear the joy of the callers and their testimonies of how the prayer line has helped them in different areas of their lives naturally and spiritually is simply amazing and adds a greater level of appreciation for the power of intercession.

In addition to calling in faithfully, they spread the word to others that they may call and experience the anointing that rests on the intercessors praying on the line.

Without a doubt, I am extremely grateful for the intercessors that the Lord has given me to help pray for others. They are genuinely anointed, and incredibly dedicated to the ministry of prayer.
Through their collective prayers we have seen body's healed, loved ones brought back from the brink of death, souls saved, and the power of God heal and restore broken lives, relationships, as well as financial situations.

I have witnessed countless occasions as individuals come on the line heavy laden, depressed or despondent and leave refreshed and rejoicing in the goodness of God. God has healed hearts and lives devastated by divorce, death, disease and the tragic loss of employment and/or home. It is always a rewarding experience to have people who call in need of a word of guidance or direction and the Holy Ghost brings forth a word of wisdom, prophecy or knowledge that totally transforms their entire circumstance.

There is also the tremendous blessing when, as an intercessor, you call in and you are facing issues and challenges of your own, only to have the Holy Ghost raise you above it and pour out on you as you engage Him on behalf of others.

The absolute sheer joy of my myriad of experiences since starting the Women of Faith Intercessory Prayer Line cannot adequately be described. The joy that comes from witnessing God's transforming, healing and miraculous workings through the power of prayer can only be equaled by the exceeding great rewards garnered through the years of interceding on behalf of God's precious people.

I pray that you will have these same experiences as you embark on starting your own prayer line.

Notes

Notes

CONCLUSION

The harvest in our land is truly ripe and it is those who are called to intercede who are charged to *"...pray ye therefore to the Lord, of the harvest, that he would send forth laborers into His harvest..."* Luke 10:2 KJV. Intercession is important to God and there is not a lot that we can expect Him to do or change, except someone is willing to ask of Him on behalf of others.

The bible says Jesus ever lives to make intercession for us, therefore intercession means something to God. If you have chosen to accept the call to intercede and begin an Intercessory Prayer Line make a full commitment to giving God a ministry of excellence, anointing and compassion for those for whom you will intercede.

The bible says in, 2 Peter 1:10 *"Wherefore the rather, brethren, give diligence to make your calling and election sure: for if ye do these things, ye shall never fall:*

The Intercessory Prayer Line, once you begin, will be something your callers will look forward to each day and session. Therefore, be sure the days, hours and time slots you select are what you *and* your intercessors can consistently adhere to. It is not something to be done haphazardly or if you cannot be present at the days and times you choose. ****Note: If you select early morning hours to pray be sure that you or any intercessors in charge are always fully awake, vibrant and pleasant in greeting your callers.****

People will count on you and those who serve with you to touch heaven in their behalf. Being diligent or making every effort to be faithful to the ministry undertaken is, as in other areas of our lives, very important, and yields great rewards. God always looks, with favor, upon the diligent.

God is faithful and dependable and greatly values the lives and various conditions of His people. He seeks those who will make themselves available to His Spirit to meet Him in prayer in their own lives. Then who will posture themselves to be used as intercessors for the Saints.

Dedicated individuals who stand in the place of intercession place themselves between and among God's people, His purpose and answers for them and the disruption of those plans by the enemy. It's all about His love for you, the Saints and/or the unsaved who will call your prayer line to be connected with that love and the answers His Spirit will provide.

Remember this; an intercessor is a person who by calling or by nature *chooses* to be a mediator on behalf of those who cannot intervene for themselves. We make requests, we carry requests, we urge, we plead, discuss and sacrifice, as we *make war* in the Spirit realm on behalf of others. The Holy Spirit allows us to have a powerful, supernatural impact on the final outcomes for those we serve.

There is a difference between persons who are called intercessors and a person who prays. Any person can pray, but not all praying people are intercessors. The distinction of an intercessor is hidden in their heart and life of prayer and a deep love for the Father.

The Intercessors heart is bound in *love and mercy* as they stand in the gap for others, seeking mercy in place of judgment, crying for life instead of death, hope in place of despair and releasing unspeakable joy in the face of sadness.

It is my sincere prayer that this manual has challenged **you** to *be* and *train* intercessors so powerful and yielded they can pray a prayer, make a request, make a stand, war in the Spirit and have it bear fruit for the masses.

The Lord is issuing a directive restoring the callings of intercessors to the body of Christ. He is raising up a powerful and power-filled army of volunteers, who are willing to stand in the gap and make up the hedge.

The task or assignment is *not* the reward. It is the *results*.

Notes

Notes

CONTACT:

Minister Vanessa Jackson
Email: veryblesswoman1@sbcglobal.net

Visit Vanessa Jackson on facebook

Women of Faith Prayer Ministries
P.O. Box 642
Park Forest, Illinois 60466
Prayer Line:
1-218-339-6427 passcode 7777#
Prayer Request and Comment Line:
1-206-666-9791

Women of Faith Prayer Days and Times:

Mon. and Thurs. 7:00 p.m. CST

Connect with the
Women of Faith Prayer Ministries on
Facebook

www.ingramcontent.com/pod-product-compliance
Lightning Source LLC
Chambersburg PA
CBHW081023040426
42444CB00014B/3333